Pandemonium

Pandemonium

The Rise of Predatory Locales in the Postwar World

by Branden Hookway

PUBLISHED BY
Princeton Architectural Press; Kevin C. Lippert, Publisher
37 East 7th Street, New York, NY 10003
212.995.9620

and

Rice University School of Architecture; Lars Lerup, Dean
6100 Main Street, Houston, TX 70005
713.527.4864

ISBN 1-56898-191-0

03 02 01 00 99   5 4 3 2 1

Printed and bound in Canada.

Designed by Bruce Mau Design / Studio !KAZAM
Branden Hookway, Sanford Kwinter, and Bruce Mau with Barr Gilmore

Edited by Sanford Kwinter and Bruce Mau

Cover image: *Fail-Safe* (detail), 1963 © Columbia Pictures Industries, Inc.
All rights reserved. Courtesy of Columbia Pictures; merged with a typical
landscape plan (detail), 1963-4, from the German Quickborner Team, GEG-
Versand, Kamen, Germany.

For a free catalog of books published by Princeton Architectural Press,
call 800.722.6657 or visit www.papress.com

LIBRARY OF CONGRESS CATALOGING-IN-PUBLICATION DATA
is available from the publisher

Contents

Foreword

Lars Lerup, Dean, School of Architecture

The infrastructure of the Metropolis is no longer that of the city. The repetition of buildings along perimeter blocks as shapers of streets and plazas has been superseded by pandemonia. This has killed that.

The urbanist's toolkit no longer includes the Froebel blocks of the past. For those enamored of the ordered striations of the city plan, today's suburban metropolis is utter tohubohu. Bandwidth has replaced the boulevard, and "five blocks west" has given way to the mouse click. After thousands of years of bricks held by mortar, the new Metropolis is toggled together by attention spans.

At the Rice School of Architecture, we have accepted one challenge above all others: the task of retooling. The present work represents one aspect of a broad field of speculation that we have encouraged over the years as part of our mandate to rethink the city.

Note on Design, Research and Work

Bruce Mau

Among the most difficult tasks facing design today is how to connect design to a social project. This is especially difficult because most design remains the outcome of service rendered to clients and oriented primarily to augmenting the effectiveness of messages, products and identities in a marketplace of increasing rationality and competitiveness. If designers are to free themselves from the increasingly dangerous logic of subservience it will only be by somehow contriving, here and there, to become their own clients, to become both the creators and the shapers of messages and content. Few practices however could long sustain such a demand. It has been my fortune over the years to have developed collaborative relationships with artists, writers and, in the context of Rice University, with students and researchers. My participation in the Studio !KAZAM project represents our first systematic attempt to turn design practice into a research project.

When Kwinter and I began researching the history and theory of work over a decade ago we had little idea how encompassing such a topic could become, how fully and oppressively it could devour every reflection on modern society and life. My own interest in setting up an innovative studio workplace was soon swamped by ethical and theoretical considerations that in time I realized could only be dealt with in the most oblique and fluid manner. It became immediately and frighteningly clear just how powerful a force design had already become in shaping our world, our attitudes, our bodies and our lives. The present collaboration with Branden Hookway, Sanford Kwinter and the Rice School of Architecture has been especially gratifying for having given preliminary shape to a field of inquiry to which my own practice has been inextricably bound.

Introduction: **War in Peace**

Sanford Kwinter

This book arose from the City-War Collective formed at Rice University in late
1994 as part of a multi-pronged initiative to establish a unique study center and
experimental lab under the wider rubric of the Rice Center for Urbanism (ReCurb).
Though the Center lasted for a mere three semesters, it produced a number of
astonishing projects of collaboration between Rice faculty and students, and in
many ways formed a model for an entirely new type of pedagogy. **Pandemonium**
is the first publication to bring the results of those intensely fertile and chaotic
months to a public beyond the campus hedges.

Our work at the Collective focused on the cryptic "renaissance" represented by
the comprehensive system of innovations in knowledge and technics that not
only surrounded the Second World War but, from a certain viewpoint, might
actually be said to have played a role in *producing* it. In industrial societies, we
surmised, politics is by no measure the only mode through which war is pursued
by "other means." Or rather, to save the sanctity of Karl von Clausewitz's beautiful
phrase, we might say that if politics in the twentieth century seems to be disap-
pearing before our very eyes, it is only because it is penetrating so intimately
into the very geometries and rhythms of knowledge itself. (The now common
phrase "knowledge industry" alone points to a stunningly rationalized commodity
relationship that was only rarely and dimly foreseen before the war yet, from
today's standpoint, marks a systematic and unambiguous transformation of
regimes.) This revolution in knowledge is, of course, none other than the information or cybernetic revolution.

The demons of **Pandemonium** descend primarily from the demons of James
Clerk-Maxwell's nineteenth-century thought experiments with heat and gases, and
the freshly discovered rule-based behaviors that determined them. It might be

said that materialism found far deeper and more reliable apologists in the nineteenth-century thermodynamicists than it did in Marx and Engels, or at least that the revolutionary social and historical "dynamicists" of the nineteenth century never dreamed to what degree their ideas depended on, and could well have been further served by, adjacent developments in the physical and life sciences. Marx saw social life as buffeted, driven and shaped by irresistible but logically ordered economic forces whose end product was assumed to be inevitable: the "catastrophic" leap to democratic equilibrium. Heat scientists likewise formulated the mysterious "second law": all closed systems lose order, all decay toward entropy. Yet for neither Marx nor Clerk-Maxwell was this simply a mechanical or energetic relation; something new had clearly emerged, a system of distributed management that could not be dissociated from the material milieus whose particles and behavioral quirks were being managed. This was the birth of information science (heat and economics), and demons are the fabulas of its deepest, most glorious, and most insidious mysteries. The demon represents the world's first glimpse of a phenomenon that earlier centuries and modes of thought could not directly face without endowing it first with John Milton's gargoyle mask. That faceless entity is the phenomenon of *control*.

Morally speaking, the world is required to present itself as the inert product of an endowing god, and if this world's pristine and original order and shape appears today degraded and unrecognizable, it is at least this "divine" order — and no other — that has been lost. Our modernity, however, as tradition sees it, is not the story of order lost, but rather of one type of order superseding another. The type of order that issues from the stuff of the world itself, the order whose cause is inseparable from the domain of its effects, has, since the time of Lucretius represented the wild and irreducible element of Nature. Yet philosophies of Nature (and immanence) fell into neglect, or became benign subjects of poetic speculation, once the powerful methods of scientific mechanism came to the fore in the seventeenth century. Today, as philosophies of Nature slowly reclaim their reign over knowledge, a broad host of changes are taking place in our world: the "wild", the vital, and the quick are once again being allowed to speak, but only the better to be harnessed and put at the service of production (capital).

Cities, economists have long argued, and not nations represent the fundamental units of the organization of production. Cities are gases that defy entropy by ceaselessly producing and accumulating wealth (order). To understand the city, we must understand the "control" structures that determine its shape and dynamics. We must see the city as a volatile gas and no longer as an inert solid. This phase shift, according to our ReCurb parlance[1], carries the name of "Metropolis." Metropolis is a cybernetic manifold of control structures — a few of which have been speculatively isolated and described in the present work. Because gases can be understood best through statistical correlations and overall global behavior, what we see happening today is the general adoption of a market model to both explain and coerce certain behaviors from social (many part) systems. (Markets, Friedrich Hayek taught, are valuable because they are smart, and smart because they distribute information efficiently — more efficiently than matter itself.)

[1] See Lars Lerup, "Stim and Dross", in **After the City**, (Cambridge: The MIT Press, 1999), Albert Pope, **Ladders**, (New York: Princeton Architectural Press, 1997), and Michael Bell and Sze Tsung Leong, "347 Years: Slow Space," in **Slow Space**, ed. Michael Bell and Sze Tsung Leong, (New York: Monacelli Press, 1998).

Discrete, autonomous physical elements are giving way today in engineering and design to phlogistons and fields, landcapes and environments, according to a seamless and seemingly irresistible logic. If, as a culture, we have become morbidly obsessed with communication, it is because the communicational ethos compels, not so much our liberty as our participation in loops of social and psychic (i.e., crypto-economic) production. Indeed, we are today forced to produce the Metropolis and are given no other choice: it is the savage and meager return for all that has been subtly and ceremoniously expropriated from us.

Even still, the story that **Pandemonium** tells may well not be a true one (yet who could offer a credible refutation?). It may be no more than a cautionary tale, a faerie story to be sure, one meant to sharpen vigilance or provoke troubled sleep. We have made no secret of our commitment to the "paranoid method" of historical investigation, or of our commitment to rooting the self in history by telling experimentally coherent stories about who we are and what we have become. In this we have tried to follow the example of certain writers — Max Weber and Michel Foucault, but preeminently Thomas Pynchon in **Gravity's Rainbow**. We offer the present work more as a model for future experiment and research than as a milestone on some already planned or anticipated highway. **Pandemonium** is a work of *affective* urbanism, meant as much to engage a reader as to disengage him/her from the exquisite servility so scrupulously fostered by contemporary metropolitan life.

Houston, February 2, 1999

Pandemonium: The Rise of Predatory Locales in the Postwar World

Branden Hookway

1. Magnetic-core RAM, developed through a coalition between MIT, the US Air Force, and the Navy known as Project Whirlwind, extended the range of machinic cognition beyond merely aiding computation, leading to the first real-time human-computer interfaces. In the 1,024 bit memory plate (of 1952) pictured here, each ferrite ring in the winding array stores a single bit, with a magnetizing coil to switch the polarization of the ring between two states (corresponding to zero or one) and a sensing coil to concurrently read this state.

Retina

Our contemporary world is driven by processes of abstraction. These processes have recently begun to generate criteria of industrial and organizational formation radically different from those to which we became accustomed during the modernist era. The advent of miniaturization in midcentury telecommunications and information processing, for example, has led to a new order of technologies that sociologist Daniel Bell has called *compunications*. In compunicational milieus, information processing begins to transpire so quickly (on the order of nanoseconds) that it is said to seem essentially timeless; thus communications networks have quickly developed to the point where information processing has become indistinguishable from the act of communication itself. The medium and, by extension, the various complex acts of mediation, for all intents and purposes, have become invisible.

Like the human eye, where through biological evolution the retina became the site on which raw visual data were both received and coded into neural impulses readable by a central nervous system, the everyday telecommunications devices to whose logic we are increasingly subjected (fax machines,

Already in 1977, Daniel Bell portrayed the trajectory of Western technological development through five trends: the *miniaturization* of electronic components; *increases in processing speed* and the resultant transformations in communications systems; *automation* through cybernetics; the unprecedented *explosion of quantity* of information itself (and the corresponding need for standardized knowledge-retrieval banks); and the *collapse of time and space* through the instantaneity of communication systems. This trajectory was formulated around problems of networking and interconnectivity, the protocol of connection language necessary for "rational cooperation" with the machine. "In that fundamental sense," Bell argued, "the space-time framework of the world oikoumene [was] set."[1]

cellular phones, Internet protocols, VCRs, etc.) are the social sites on which the selective filtering and shaping of information is taking place. This technologically mediated form of capital—information—has long since become a global lingua franca: What system of border controls could halt the flow of information, a substance that could never appear "foreign" because it is by definition already reconstituted as universal?

The collective machinic, or technological vision machine, becomes a tool not just for gathering information, but for giving it form—for locating all information within the realm of technological reproduction and simultaneous transmission. Indeed, the volume of information generated through the massive increases in computing power and data-collection devices has forced a radical shift in the processes of communication and control, one centered on the problem of filtering information for valuable data. Originally a program of military intelligence analysts dealing with the logistics of processing the explosion of information generated in battle, today the filtering imperative belongs to our entire social-industrial system.

The Keynesian model began to plummet as an article of faith in macro-economic circles during the years of the Vietnam War. This chute was accelerated by a series of economic crises beginning in the late 1960s and characterized by widespread social unrest, followed by a shortage of raw materials, rising inflation, and economic stagnation. These crises have taken two broad forms. Michael Piore and Charles Sabel refer to the first as a "regulation crisis," resulting from a disruption of the balancing mechanisms connecting production and consumption. They derive (but at the same time differentiate) the term from the French *régulation*, which connotes regulation not in terms of external control (in the sense of governmental regulation) but as an internal "balancing mechanism," or "equilibration."[2] It is in this sense of self-equilibration that neoclassical economic theory (and the 19th-century marginalist theory from which it is derived) views the functioning of the market. The second, and less obvious, form of crisis concerns what Lewis Mumford referred to as technics, or the sum of methods and means used in production. This type of crisis admits that a change in mode of production affects far more than the way goods are produced; it is a change in the very substance of society itself, in its generalized systems of exchange, in the "abstract diagrams" through which elements and processes are conceived of, interrelated, and subsequently directed. The Keynesian model, and the state-regulated capitalism enacted throughout the developed countries of the West, had sought to mitigate crises in the economic system that had developed around mass-production technologies.[3]

Capitalism itself is shifting in response to this and other crises of information. Modern capital is almost no longer at all embodied in Fordist mass production, or Keynesian supply-and-demand equations. It has shifted to a military-style economy (the extension of platoon-style hierarchies into the economy, the on-going interweaving of domestic and military institutions) in which the goal is the mobilization of forces—productive, consumptive, and structural—and the continued acceleration of progress. The Keynesian shibboleth of wage-driven consumption, organized around the macroeconomic concept of equilibrium and promoting equality between wage increases and marginal labor productivi-ty, has shifted to a scenario in which productivity is increasingly divorced from

2. While the cadres of the Vietnamese Revolutionary Army blended seemlessly with the soldiers on the battlefield, the overly-centralized US command mostly saw the war through the abstraction of numbers, losing touch with the actual conditions of the war. After the Tet offen-sive of 1968, the US chain of command began to break down. This attenuation expressed itself in racism, drug use, and, most radically, in the practice of fragging: the attempt by men on the field to kill their commanding officer, generally using a grenade, rather than follow a reckless or dangerous command. It was as though the chain of com-mand had turned in on itself, forcibly decentralizing itself, by injecting into the hierarchy a certain negative fluidity.

3. Renouncing the sovereign self in the tumult of the crowd. Mosh pit as superorganism: Rage Against the Machine, Rock am Ring Festival, Germany 1996.

labor. The market comes to be seen as merely an accelerator of forces, a facilitator of constant growth and expansion.

In this sea change within capitalist organization, a useful distinction may be made between "citadels" and "environments." Citadels form coherent, distinct entities characterized by distance and external control over their agents. The subject of history has traditionally been that of citadels, whether in the form of states, cities, production processes, or egos. Within environments, by contrast, control is endogenous, and the relationship of controller and controllee is one of intimacy or closeness. One is not made a subject to an environment, one is rather *enslaved* within it—absorbed and redefined as an integrated, productive

"Closeness" describes the relative dissolution of the formal relationships between two entities. Without this formal relationship, the message and the medium are reconstituted beneath the skin; received in a state of distraction, like a waking dream. "The equipment-free aspect of reality here has become the height of artifice; the sight of immediate reality has become an orchid in the land of technology." For Walter Benjamin, what has been lost is the "unique existence of things," the existential presence or "aura," that requires a view from outside. The mass-reproduction techniques of the art object, culminating in film, frees the object from tradition, and follows society's desire to surround itself with the likenesses of things. Yet at a time when the manufacture of identity is a motive force of the economy (the proliferation of branded and blue-chip culture), *aura has not truly disappeared*; instead, it has become mobile, "liquidated" only in the sense of "made fluid." Aura is performative, and like information, it is defined not by its substance but by the effects it produces, by the way that it closes a circuit, embeds—subsumes—two entities within a channeled relationship. The substance of aura—its identity—is then capable of any sort of transformation, since it is no longer grounded in a static metaphysic. It is itself embedded within an environment, a field, through which value and substance are constantly shifting, a network of fragmentary existences through which even apparently subversive activity may be directed. Benjamin's "universal equivalence of things" can only be a universality of capture, leading to homogeneity within connection protocol and often cloaked beneath supposed difference.[4]

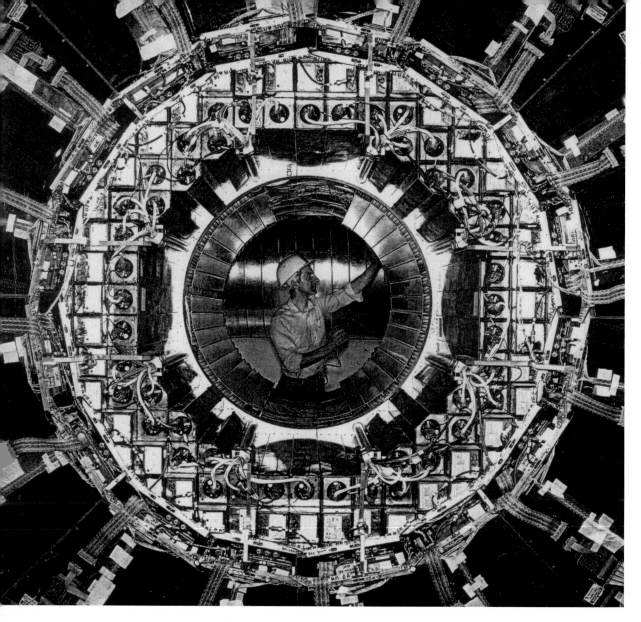

4. Through the compunicational looking-glass: new decentralized, environmental techniques of social control situate Man within an encompassing techno-economic reality. This new organizational imperative can be said to be infiltrating all fields of human endeavor: Artificial Intelligence in the cognitive sciences and philosophy of the mind, the new realization of the potentials and extensions of markets and market institutions (i.e., computer-aided arbitrage and advanced credit institutions, and the realization of the bounded or heuristic rationality of decision-making and the coefficient of informational in economics; new techniques for harvesting the nervous apparatus of workers in Post- or neo-Fordist organization; in the relation between labor and machines following the use of cybernetic and informational technologies; and finally in the playing out of this milieu of production in the formation of place, from the office and factory to the reorganization of urban and even global fabrics along the new imperatives of communication flow.

part. As such, regulation within environments does not require the presence of a "centralized" force, such as a dominant ideology or a police state. In fact, such regulation hampers the central power dynamic of the environment.

The history of the late 20th century can be seen globally as the surreptitious replacement of citadels—which tend to restrict the flow of information—by less viscous environments, and the subsumption of information within capital. This movement of capital's sphere of power expands externally and internally at once, invading previously unknown territories while progressively parsing those factors over which it already has control. This new techno-economic regime can be imagined as an ever-alert eye constantly scanning the environment for information that may be valorized, producing market environments wherever they emerge and at the very moment of their apprehension. This generalized vigilance can truly be called predatory in nature, for it activates everything it apprehends with a view simply to seizing it. It may be understood as a Pandemonic Eye.

The notion of the Pandemonic Eye conveys the properties and movements of the technics of control within a general regime of decentralizing processes, though with the caveat that decentralization is constituted only within a more comprehensive hidden recentralization. The movement toward decentralization (toward the cyborg, for example) does not lead to absolute liberation, as is often claimed. In the same way, the postmodern shift toward multiplicity, toward the blurring of subject and object, is not itself immune to the operation of power: this theoretical shift was in many ways preceded by the evolution of power structures which use strikingly similar techniques of control. Just as the phenomenological camera eye captures and deploys information in a way entirely specific to the medium of film, so the Pandemonic Eye, and the technological development which it represents, works along characteristic lines of development, in the formation of the specific milieu that it engenders.

Protocol

What is pandemonium? The word suggests chaotically activated surfaces, a swirl of constant motion, even brutal ubiquitous insurrection. In any case, it is a chaos not without intentionality, efficacy, or essential properties. Literally, it is an environment of "all demons," an environment made animate through daimons, the emissaries in classical thought between the gods and man who were beyond human control, unbalancing the careful plans of men: a sort of diabolic friction between heaven and earth. During the Renaissance pandemonium was said to emerge from the sleep of reason, to pose a threat of excess, superstition, a manifestation of the disorder seething behind the cool, Platonic edifice. The battle between the two realms was constant.

Today the emergence of so-called compunications and the new informational economy paradoxically signals the rationalist triumph of the old pandemonic forms of organization over the staid citadels of the old reason. The shift is occurring across the spectrum of information technologies as we move from models of the global application of intelligence, with their universality and frictionless dispersal, to one of local applications, where intelligence is site-specific

5. The Homeric daimon emphasized the actions (as opposed to the theos, or personality) of the gods, so that daimons became associated with Fate, with contingency and sudden supernatural interventions as opposed to reason and clarity. Milton's Pandemonium or capitol of Hell was the realm of angels who distorted the perfect clarity of the Word of God. Illustration by Gustav Doré for Milton's Paradise Lost.

and fluid. The mechanistic universe, the universe of discrete parts, has long since been abandoned, and questions of taxonomy and classification (which con- sititute, perhaps, a science of *distance*) are fading in relevance to the search for patterns in the behavior of systems. Instead, the signature technique of the late 20th century has become the computer simulation. The simulation is not meant to specify unknown variables in a mechanistic sense; its power lies in finding similarities or analogies *across time* in complex processes for which the precise actions of variables remain unknown. The simulation forsakes the unspecified interaction of constitutive variables in favor of making visible larger environmen- tal patterns. Today, the type of information which is most valuable is irreducibly embedded within an ever-changing environment, from the interactions of institu- tions in a market to the interactions of neurons in a human brain.

6. Tank simulator, US Army
7. Tank gunner, Vietnam

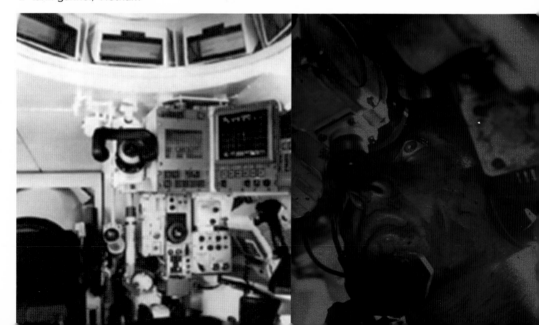

With the need and the newly acquired ability to generate and deploy unprecedented amounts of information came the logistical problem of how to filter that information, how to discern patterns within the torrents of data. For serial computer architectures, which process information sequentially at the level of bits (the binary digit, the primal yes/no, A/not-A of classical symbolic logic), the capacity to perceive patterns is limited. While such machines are capable of incredible feats of arithmetical number-crunching, they are virtually unable to filter environmental data in any useful way. The cognitive capacities of sequential architectures can thus be easily distinguished from human cognition, which relies on abstracting the relevent developmental patterns from a continuous flow of sense-perceptions. The solution to the problem of complex, adaptive machine perception lies in pandemonium-based architectures.

Filtering is a central concern in the problem of control within distributed systems. A filter works by identifying patterns or signatures within raw or previously unorganized data. As automatic filters become more sophisticated, vaster and more disparate sets of data may be subjected to analysis and mined for useful information, making possible increasingly far-ranging techniques of information gathering. As Manuel DeLanda has shown, this two-pronged evolution of information technology has led to the generation of vast amounts of information through "vacuum cleaner" methods, to which an "intelligence analyst" applies techniques of pattern recognition. For the US government, the vanguard of intelligence-gathering techniques have congealed around the vacuum-cleaner approach used by two large bureaucratic agencies specializing in different media: photoanalysis at the CIA and cryptoanalysis at the National Security Agency (NSA). The NSA believes it must stay five years ahead of the state of the art in commercial information technology. The technically sophisticated combination of exhaustive intelligence-gathering techniques and methods of data filtering and analysis based on electromagnetic media led DeLanda to coin the term Panspectron: "There are many differences between the Panopticon [of Jeremy Bentham] and the Panspectron being assembled at the NSA. Instead of positioning some human bodies around a central sensor, a multiplicity of sensors is deployed around all bodies: its antenna farms, spy satellites and cable-traffic intercepts feed into its computers all the information that can be gathered. This then is processed through a series of 'filters' or keyword watchlists. The Panspectron does not merely select certain bodies and certain (visual) data about them. Rather, it compiles information about all at the same time, using computers to select the segments of data relevant to its surveillance tasks."[5]

A pandemonium, or massively parallel, computer architecture consists of a multitude of quasi-independent interconnected software agents—demons—which operate simultaneously. In the case of an early pandemonium model (c. 1960) designed to recognize hand-printed letters, one demon, for example, would be assigned the task of recognizing horizontal strokes, emitting a "shriek" whose intensity varies in proportion to how closely the data fit its search and decision-making criteria (i.e., more loudly when it encounters the letters A or T, less so with O or S). At the next hierarchical level, a cognitive demon would be attentive to the shrieks of the demon population below it and would assign a value based on the relative "weights" or intensities of the shrieks. Other demons would simultaneously perform disparate tasks at the same level, subjecting the letter to grids of various kinds, and the data they gathered would continually funnel up the demon hierarchy, until, finally, a judgment of some sort would be made.

In this way, the data set or environment inhabited by the pandemonium model is rendered globally active through the busy presence of the demons.

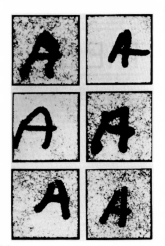

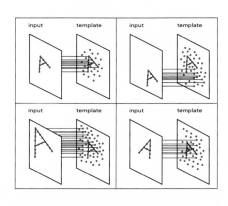

8. Letter forms easily recognized by the human mind.
9. Pattern recognition through template-matching bears little in common with human cognition.

The demon's quasi-autonomous nature enables them to act with a certain kind of limited initiative; that is they can become activated by and run their subprograms based on environmental cues rather than obeisance to a direct command from a central processing unit. The demon is a potentiality, like an enzyme, that roams across an environment until triggered into action by an informational or environmental cue.

In contrast to a rigid, vertical hierarchy of serial architectures, where decisions are processed one at a time by a central processing unit, pandemonium architectures process multiple levels of information simultaneously. The latter thus allows for behaviors which often appear more intuitive than programmed, more fluid in operation, more sensitive to environmental data, and, most significantly, capable of learning from experience. The ability to process information in a way analogous to biological structures opens up new domains for the Pandemonic Eye; within the realm of information processing there now exists the ability to filter data in a way which approaches the scope of "wet systems" like human cognition.

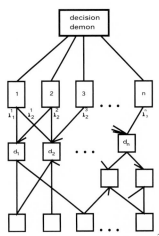

10. A pandemonium architecture (1960) for letter recognition runs a number of subprograms (demons) simultaneously, such as counting the number of downstrokes that would cross a series of horizontal lines, whose results are filtered up the demon hierarchy.
11. A Pandemonium is not a tree: Note the interconnections of subprograms. Original diagram of pandemonium architecture (1958).

12. Jackson Pollock painting Number 32, 1950. ph. Hans Nemuth.
13. Jackson Pollock worked in continuous feedback thought and bodily movement, eye and hand, body and brain, locked together in a simultaneous heated exercise of decision and sensation. Here, the surrealist rendering of slit-like eyes underscores the resolve to obliterate discrete forms in favor of an "all-over" or environmental apprehension of space out of which patterns are generated or recognized. The pour technique was adopted shortly after "Eyes in the Heat," in an attempt to obliterate the boundaries of his painting, to paint without beginning or end, to "literally be in the painting." "Eyes in the Heat," 1946, oil on canvas, 54 x 43 inches, Guggenheim Collection, NY.

For Oliver Selfridge, the original theorist of the pandemonium model of computer architecture, sequential processing (or von Neumann architecture) is "more natural for the machine" but requires elaborate checking and back-tracking procedures when dealing with "noisy" situations that go beyond simple and reasonable dichotomies. Processing data as the human mind does requires a parallel processing computer architecture, where "all the questions are asked at once, and the answers presented simultaneously to the decision-maker."[6] The von Neumann bottleneck—data passing bit by bit through a central processing unit—is far removed from the complexity of human learning.

Daniel Dennett, among others, has used pandemonium models to explain human cognition: The specialist demons "are often opportunistically enlisted in new roles, for which their narrative talents more or less suit them. The result is not bedlam only because the trends that are imposed on all this activity are themselves the product of design. Some of this design is innate, and is shared with other animals. But it is augmented, and sometimes even overwhelmed in importance, by microhabitats of thought that are developed in the individual, partly idiosyncratic results of self-exploration and partly the predesigned gifts of culture. Thousands of memes, mostly born by language, but also by wordless 'images' and other data structures, take up residence in an individual brain, shaping its tendencies and thereby turning it into a mind."[7]

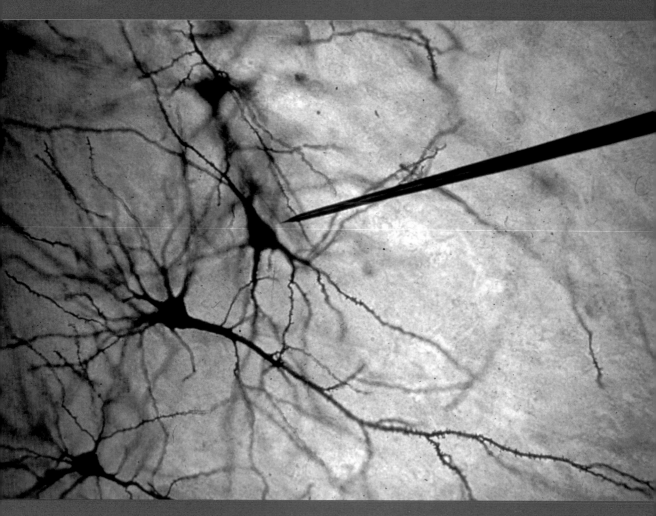

14. Neurons with probe.

Neuron

The history of artificial intelligence is inseparable from developments in neuroscience and in information theory in general; breakthroughs in one field have found immediate correlations in the others. Newly founded disciplines, such as cognitive psychology, have served to increase the links between these disciplines, further blurring the distinction between machinic and human cognition.

The pandemonium model itself arises from the locus of several fields, combining concepts from the neurosciences, cybernetics, administrative sciences, and human information processing. The driving force behind the convergence of these fields was military application. Armies and their command systems needed to be able to deploy the avalanches of information generated in any modern battlefield situation. Oliver Selfridge, for example, an assistant at MIT to cybernetic pioneer Norbert Weiner, developed his pandemonium model while working at the RAND Corporation and at Lincoln Lab, a high-security research institute associated with both the Army and MIT.

15. MIT's role as a leading military research center began during the second World War at which time it was primarily engaged in the development of radar systems. The radomes on MIT's Building 6 became the symbol for generations to come of MIT's involvement in war research.

16. Originally conceived of by the Air Force in 1945 as an analog flight simulator, MIT's Whirlwind computer would become the fastest general purpose digital computer of its time. Whirlwind would be applied to such problems as flight control and the coordination of the first networked early warning radar system, SAGE.

The establishment of institutions like the RAND Corporation and the Lincoln Laboratory at the close of World War II reflects the military's realization of the escalating importance of pioneering new technologies, tactics, and, in short, deployments of information in warfare, both hot and cold. Encouraged by the success of wartime projects like the Manhattan Project and the MIT Radiation Laboratory, the military sought to further harness cutting-edge academic speculation and experimentation, along with the productive power of industry, to its own directives. Project RAND (from "research and development") had its beginnings in a contract between the Army Air Force and Douglas Aircraft Company in 1946. Founded as "a program of study and research on the broad subject of intercontinental warfare other than surface," to recommend "preferred techniques and instrumentalities," it brought academics and scientists into contact with a number of government departments and private corporations. An Air Force officer summarized succinctly what the Air Force sought to gain: "Because of the diversity of skills and knowledge required to cope with current

and future problems of national security, and because of the interest which all on the research staff share in the solutions of these problems, an organization like RAND represents one (rare) device for overcoming the increasing compartmentalization and specialization of knowledge."

The realization that policy decisions and technology are inseparable led to the creation of a totally new type of institution: "We had to fit into existing molds. For example, the Douglas Company did not have an existing job description for a philosopher. By reading the job-salary table backward, we discovered he was Design Specialist A." RAND took on an astoundingly diverse set of issues, including policy research (especially the formulation of a deterrence strategy in the Cold War), strategic air bases and air defense systems, nuclear weapons and weapon strategy, communications and satellite systems, and missiles and space warfare. It conducted research on project cost analysis and the logistics of transport and information processing, economic and political policy, systems analysis ("choice among alternative future systems, where degrees of freedom and uncertainties are large"),

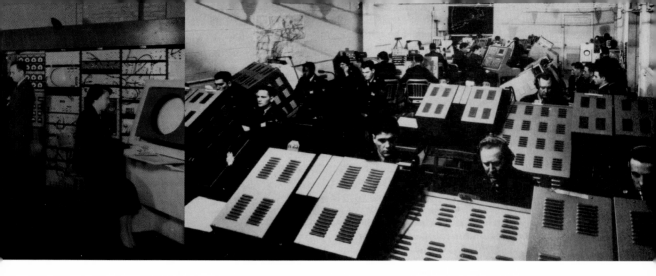

17. Military funding of SAGE (for Semi-Automatic Ground Environment) began after the Soviet nuclear bomb tests of 1949, to guard against a surprise bomber attack over the North Pole through the creation of a comprehensive system to track planes and chart intercept routes. Twenty-three stations (plus an experimental station at Lincoln Lab) were built in bombproof shelters in the US and Canada, each using a Whirlwind-type computer to coordinate incoming data from a comprehensive network of radars and other sources. The real-time nature of this data made interface design a vital problem; in this 1953 prototype of SAGE, Air Force officers monitor the northern skies on early, TV-like computer monitors.

meteorology, and game theory (applied to Cold War issues). Its projects on mathematics give one a sense of the broadness of its research: "For example, the problem of efficient assignment of targets to aircraft leads to advances in methods of decentralized planning in a large-scale organization." RAND also carried out pioneering work on the uses of computers (including work on heuristics and the development of efficient command and control systems). In its first 15 years, over one million copies of 7,000 RAND publications (from technical papers to books) were distributed; this total, of course, doesn't begin to reflect the amount of work that was considered classified.[8]

The Lincoln Laboratory was founded in 1950 out of MIT's great wartime research center, the Radiation Laboratory. Funded by the Army and Navy, the Rad Lab became best known for inventing and producing radar equipment for both aerial and sea warfare. Much like the Rad Lab, Lincoln Labs included a number of divisions (including Communications and Components, Long-Range Communications, Secure Communications, Aircraft Control and Warning, and the Digital Computer Laboratory), with a continuous

transfer of expertise and technology across these departments required by the military projects it took on. While funding came from military sources, Lincoln Labs worked extensively with industry, including IBM, Bell Telephone Laboratories, the Western Electric Company, Convair, Hughes Aircraft, Raytheon, and Jackson and Moorland. Projects of the 1950s included NOMAC (Noise Modulation and Correlation), which led to technologies of secure military transmissions through the use of noise signals (spread so thin as to escape notice) and the development of an air defense system based along an extensive network of radar. This "electronic fence" (the project, called SAGE, or Semi-Automatic Ground Environment, involved consultation with RAND) made use of one of the earliest computers, the Whirlwind. While these projects employed MIT faculty and graduate students, the work was highly classified, and in 1952 Lincoln Labs moved off campus to better ensure its privacy.

MIT's entry into what Eisenhower called the military-industrial complex forced the school to radically alter its method of operation. James Killian, president of

MIT from 1949 to 1959, noted that "there were times when both labs [Lincoln Labs and the similar Instrumentation Laboratory] posed problems for us that gave us concern about their future impact on MIT....These big labs are not without their complications. For one thing, they tend to have an inflationary effect on the institutions. And when, for instance, the Instrumentation Laboratory philosophy of cradle-to-grave development began to involve the Institute in contracting with industry for many elements, we thought these presented inappropriate kinds of decisions for an academic institution." In the 1968–69 academic year, the Instrumentation Laboratory received $54.6 million in external funding, mostly from the Department of Defense (DOD) and NASA, while Lincoln Labs received $66.8 million. At the same time, on-campus sponsored research totaled $55.8 million, only 27 percent of which was DOD related.

The changing face of MIT can be seen through a comparison with prewar conditions: from the academic years 1938–39 to 1968–69, total sponsored research increased from $18,932 to $171,294,000. The ratio of faculty to undergraduates nearly doubled (from 1:8.5 to 1:4.4), while the ratio of graduate students to undergraduates more than tripled (1:3.5 to 1:1). The blurring of academic, military, and industrial realms was justified through an appeal to national defense; Julius Stratton, who became president of MIT in 1959, reported on MIT's policy toward Lincoln Labs: "The Institute has always accepted sponsored research projects as an integral part of its educational system. Such work, whether on campus or in the defense laboratories, provides unusual opportunities for both graduate students and faculty to participate in research at the frontiers of their respective fields. We recognize also that urgent demands will be made upon our resources in times, such as the present, when the safety and strength of the free world depend so greatly on advanced science and technology."[9]

18. The funding of war-research projects at MIT was set back by the growing unrest of students and faculty, culminating in the widely publicized "November Actions" of 1969 which targeted research on missile guidance systems at the Instrumentation Laboratory. As a result of these protests, MIT divested its control of the I-Lab, while the military grew more wary of engaging university laboratories in high security research.

19. The insect-like robots of Rodney Brooks evolve their ant-like gait. This "bottom-up" approach to AI contrasts with attempts to mimic human high-level functions (such as playing chess) by programming into the machine a model of the world; these robots instead interact directly with the environment around them to generate low-level behaviors (such as balancing) based on their own sensorimotor functions. For Brooks, true cognition must be both embodied in sensorimotor functions and situated in surrounding factors, biological and cultural. As in Simon's economics, "the world is its own best model."

Also at RAND was Herbert Simon, whose work in industrial administration led directly to concepts central to the development of intelligent machines; he co-wrote what is now widely considered to be the first artificial intelligence program, the Logic Theorist, in 1955. Simon argued that the search for maximizing alternatives by economic decision makers necessarily requires the expenditure of time and energy. Unlike the notion of instrumental rationality (far too often taken as an essential and unchanging component of modernity), which presumes that decision makers have access to the optimal arrangement of means to a given end, to the greatest possible efficiency and utility, Simon's theory of bounded rationality urged one instead to consider ways in which the flow of information could be made less viscous through selective channeling. Simon's idea was the decisive step toward what has come to be known as *heuristics*, the rules-of-thumb according to which people make decisions without becoming immobilized in the process by considering every possible aspect of a problem. This more fluid approach could be applied to all forms of organization, from the wiring of computers to the behavior of large institu-

Simon advocated a type of rationality that is distributed throughout the environment within which the decision-maker is situated. He denied the possibility of a rational, privileged view above the economic fray: "However adaptive the behavior of organisms in learning and choice situations, this adaptiveness falls far short of the ideal of 'maximizing' postulated in economic theory. Organisms adapt well enough to 'satisfice'; they do not, in general 'optimize.' If this is the case, a great deal can be learned about rational decision making by taking into account, at the outset, the limitations upon the capacities and complexity of the organism and by taking account of the fact that the environments to which it must adapt possess properties that permit further simplification of its choice mechanisms."[10]

tions in a market environment (Simon won a Nobel Prize in economics for this work). Much like the reconfiguration of the modern army from tight, centralized formations into the decentralized radio-linked platoons of World War II, social and industrial organizations are now urged to give up the idea of operating toward a global set of objectives, turning by contrast to the use of subgoals to allow a far more supple response to complex situations. These subgoals are then united into the larger goals of the organization in a way similar to pandemonium architecture.

But at the center of these information-processing systems, whether in the hardware of a computer or the bureaucratic structure of a transnational corporation, is the model of the neuron. Most major information-technologies advances have involved speculations as to the functioning of the nervous system. What is the secret behind the brain's ability to take neurons, which are five to six orders of magnitude slower than silicon logic gates, and assemble them in such a way as to perform certain operations many times faster than any digital computer?

The dream of information technologists is to render all surfaces active and massively parallel. These surfaces should all be capable of instant modification through the modularity of their parts and the flexibility of their pathways, and they should form a totally malleable environment with respect to facilitating the flow of information. This goal requires that citadel structures (labor unions, city grids, the skills of the artisan, and, in sum, all things which provide insoluble, grave, and singular units resistant to processes of abstraction) be liquidated and reconstituted within information capital.

The neuron model of organization is fast becoming a cultural and technological imperative thanks to the synthesis of compunications systems and the emerging global market economy. The task of the model is to reformulate the world, to learn from and translate the world into its own abstract vocabulary. Through the operation of the Pandemonic Eye, constantly scanning the boundaries of its territory, transforming and absorbing all that it apprehends, the regime of abstraction is expanded, and the directed fluidity of information, the speed of its apprehension and deployment, is increased.

20. "In the Penal Colony," after Franz Kafka. Les Machines célibataires exhibition, Paris 1977. Curator Harold Szeeman.

21. MIT's experimental milling machine, 1952.

Paraboloid

The liberation of information-processing techniques from the human body entered industrial production in the 1970s through the adoption of neo-Fordist principles, or flexible specialization. Where under the Fordist regime of the semi-automatic assembly line the rhythms of production were dependent on the rhythms of labor, the arrival of cybernetic machines, servo-devices, and numerical control severed that connection. Within this new regime, the worker is absorbed—subsumed—into the matrix of production as part of a machine-human apparatus. Both humans and machines now function as relays in an environment of total production.

In the cybernetic age, the machinist no longer uses the machine as a tool; rather, the machine is engaged in a dance of mutual surveillance. A critical step in this process was the development of numerical control (N/C), a term coined by two engineers (William M. Pease, James O. McDonough) at MIT's Servomechanism Lab. The first N/C device was a three-axis milling machine

Among the principal tasks of the early-20th-century "scientific" management of labor was to choreograph labor to the movements of simple machines, abstracting the skills of craftsmen into routines that could be quantified, diagrammed, and repeated. The implementation of cybernetic and continuous-process production in the second half of the century has made far more supple techniques of labor control necessary, extending the inherently modern processes of abstraction along cybernetic rather than merely mechanistic lines. As a result, methods of social control wielded in the old mass-production economy have been superseded by a wholly new system. Gilles Deleuze and Félix Guattari illustrate this condition by distinguishing between the "social subjection" analyzed by Marx, in which the worker is a free subject to capitalism under the wage relation, and an emergent system of "machinic enslavement." Yet machinic enslavement was actually first a property of archaic empires (what Lewis Mumford called mega-machines), in which human beings were constituent parts of a mechanism controlled by a higher entity. On the other hand, through the formal structure of the wage relation, where naked labor comes into contact with capital, the worker is exterior to the tool used and to the labor process itself. Under machinic enslavement, the relation between the force of production and the worker is characterized by closeness (immanence, unlike social subjection, which is characterized by distance). For Deleuze and Guattari, the advent of cybernetics and communications technologies has led to the formation of a third condition, a technologically sophisticated megamachine. "If motorized machines constituted the second age of the

technical machine, cybernetic and informational machines form a third age that reconstructs a generalized regime of subjection: recurrent and reversible 'humans-machines systems' replace the old recurrent and nonreversible relations of subjection between the two elements; the relation between human and machine is based on internal, mutual communication, and no longer on usage and action."[11]

This shift can be seen in the formation of sites of production at all scales. The third age of the machine—and the continuous process industries and information-technology manufacturing that now dominate the industrial landscape—has liquidated what Jean-Paul Gaudamar refered to as the "factory-fortress," the old site of social subjection. While the factory has in some cases grown more concentrated, accentuating the possibilities of large scale production, and in others become dispersed into a matrix of producers, suppliers, and subcontractors, this double movement of concentration and dispersion works to increase the mobility and fluidity of production factors, ensuring a more supple fit to market demands.

This double movement provides the context for the often discussed schism between skilled and unskilled workers. As the brunt of labor in information-technology manufacturing is automated, we have seen, on one hand, the privileging of those technically skilled workers and system analysts who control and maintain the machinery, and on the other, the growing pool of unskilled workers, whose only asset is their mobility. This change is reflected on a global scale as well, as whole nations become equivalents of mobile unskilled labor, useful only to the global market for cheap routinized labor or the export of raw materials, under the auspices of a comprador capitalism. Gaudamar asks (and this question applies on the factory floor as well as it does in a globalized market): "Is the fate of the worker thus tied to a future in which only two possibilities remain: to be a controller of flux or an element of flux?"[12]

22. The Falcon loom used what was in effect digital media, with rectangular punched cards, chained in a loop, each card representing one
shedding motion of the loom, the binary language of perforation
determining which warp threads are drawn and thus the pattern of
the weave. This process was made both fully automatic and practical
by Jacquard. While the Jacquard loom still required the presence of a
weaver, the intelligence of the process had migrated into the programming of the punched cards, thus maximizing the control of the
designer and making of the weaver merely a minder of the loom.

23. Paris, May 1968.

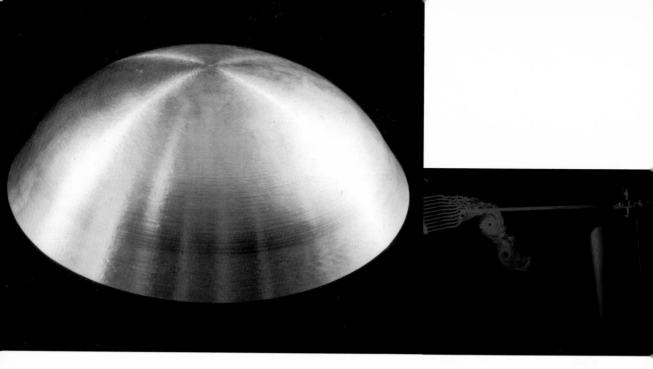

24. The first object milled on MIT's N/C milling machine was a sub-assembly for a radar lens, to be used by the Antenna Laboratory of the Air Force's Cambridge Research Center.

25. The design and manufacture of helicopter rotors are complicated by the demands of aerodynamics. A helicopter will experience four distinct wake states depending on its rate of decent, hover, or climb. Also, the loading of a rotor blade across its span is greatest at its tip because of the tip vortex, as seen in this wind-tunnel visualization.

Among the earliest numerically controlled machines were textile looms, such as the Falcon (1728) and the Jacquard (1805). Until the 20th century, the technology of numerical control was used only for novelty items such as player pianos. The invention of cybernetic technology, however, which united feedback control with information theory, pushed numerical control toward its capital-intensive, computer-based paradigm. The Parsons Corporation, headed by John T. Parsons, the son of a machinist, was the country's largest manufacturer of helicopter rotor blades in the 1940s. Rotor blades are difficult to design: unlike an airplane propellor, they do not follow a fixed plane of rotation, but constantly change pitch during revolutions around a mobile hinge that must also be structurally able to carry the weight of the helicopter.

Typically, it took a full person-year to design a single rotor blade. In 1947, after receiving an Air Force contract which would have required an enormous number of tedious calculations, Parsons found that with a rented IBM business tabulating machine he could run the calculations for a rotor in a matter of days. Further, the computer could generate an extra number of Cartesian points along the curve of the rotor which could be used as guidepoints for a jig boring mill. The rotor could then be filed down to the guidepoints, simultaneously allowing greater accuracy and decreasing the skill necessary on the part of the machinist. In appreciation, the Air Force awarded the Parsons Corporation a contract in partnership with IBM, and later MIT's Servomechanism Laboratory, to develop the technology.

(operating along the *x*, *y*, and *z* coordinates) that received its commands through punched paper tape. Three hydraulic power servo-mechanisms were used to replace the hand-operated controls of a standard milling machine. These servos received simultaneous but distinct commands from a computer (the director) connected electronically to the milling machine. The director read the binary input on the punched tape, converted the numerical code into electronic pulse trains for each space coordinate, and finally converted these pulse trains into angular positions for the three servos. The machine was completed in March 1952 and first implemented in factories in 1953. By 1960, a machine tool show in Chicago featured nearly 100 N/C units. The N/C marked the computer's foray on the factory floor, as well as the first case of purely digital information being used to shape real objects.

MIT's Servo Lab was established in 1940 as an outgrowth of a Navy program for developing accurate and rapid gun positioning on ships. The Lab became occupied with developing a general purpose digital computer, the Whirlwind, while working on a Navy contract for flight simulators. MIT gradually took control of the project from Parsons, which had been interested solely in finding a solution to a manufacturing problem, and began to entertain the possibilities of using digital control to automate the machining process.[13] "Entranced by the possibilities of full continuous path control, Pease and McDonough, the project leaders, quickly transcended the original problem—automatic machining of wing panel surfaces—to contemplate an even more general, ambitious, and elaborate application. They imagined a continuous path system for controlling three axes of motion simultaneously, in synchronization, to carve out, sculpt from solid material, any mathematically defined surface." This transformation in goals—from that of solving specific technical problems using computing as a tool, to elaborating a system in which computers could ensure total control for the design engineer—illustrates, according to historian David Noble, the effects of a marriage of technocratic academics, interested in furthering their "scientific and institutional interests," with the driving force of military prerogatives.[14]

The elliptical paraboloid pictured here was milled using an experimental N/C programming language at MIT in 1962. The surface markings are exaggerated to show cutting vectors. The 3-D spiral-cut pattern is computer-generated from a mathematical description; for all previous N/C protocols, each cutting vector would have been programmed separately. Although created under strict technological imperatives to demonstrate how this early form of computer modeling could reduce programming time (only six additional commands beyond those necessary to describe the 2-D elliptical base were needed to sculpt the 3-D object), the paraboloid has a seductive sculptural power, a resonance perhaps derived from the new type of blurring that it represents between idea and matter. Its absolute reproducibility places it firmly within the great enterprise of abstraction, and the universal exchangeability of things engendered by this enterprise. N/C was developed primarily through a joint research venture between MIT and the Air Force, which was searching for a way to increase control over the machining of airplane components. In 1957, the Air Force deputy chief of staff for materiel stated that "heretofore, regardless of how carefully drawn and specified

26. The object to the right was milled using a modified version of APT (Automatically Programmed Tools), one of the earliest high-level programming languages. Using APT, the operator would not have to learn binary code to program the machine but could rather use the English-like commands of a hierarchically structured computer language, to be compiled as code by the computer itself. APT was created at MIT between 1956-59, becoming the N/C industry standard in 1974, providing one more step in the gradual subsumption of the vocabulary of the manufacturing process, as well as in the descriptive translation of three-dimensional objects, into the dynamics of information processing.

on paper, a finished piece [of machinery] could not be any better than the machinist's interpretations." N/C delivered maximal control of the machine to management: "Since specifications are converted to objective digital codes of electronic impulses, the element of judgment is limited to that of the design engineer alone."

Management desire for the level of control possible with complete digitalization can be seen in the rejection of an alternate technology called record playback (R/P), which was both less expensive and more reliable than N/C. The R/P system used an analog tape to record the motions of a machinist at a lathe, and the playback of the tape permitted the same motions to be executed in subsequent iterations of the process. R/P technology, though full of nuance, failed to reduce fluid geometry to discrete numbers; in other words, it was guilty of permitting the individual machinist's specialized knowledge to remain in the loop.

Numerical control has had an unmistakably military flavor throughout its history, thanks to the importance of the Air Force in the early stages of its development. The military influence transcends specific technological developments, however, inciting and defining further development along various trajectories responding to military preoccupations. These preoccupations—specifically, performance, command, and modern methods—have become critically embedded within the broader methodologies and directions of industrial research in the United States. "Performance" includes meeting objectives through the use of integrated systems following the "uniformity principle." Integrated systems, which rely on interchangeable parts and highly abstracted forms of labor, allow the fast turnaround times in production that the military argues is necessary for national survival. "Control" expresses the desire to shorten chains of command, to decrease the amount of intervention between order and execution. "Modern methods" conveys the military's consistent preference for high-tech solutions, and hence, capital-intensive production.[15]

"Record-playback" differs from numerical control both in preserving the need for a pool of highly skilled machinists and in lending itself to programming on the shop floor rather than in offices under management control. With R/P, the skill of the machinist, the ability to make subtle adjustments based on intuitions about materials, is enhanced and extended. In computerized numerical control, each specific material and machine event must be translated into often dauntingly complex algorithms. One solution to this problem involves increasing capital expenditure in creating a machinic cognition capable of employing algorithms much like heuristics.

27. Project MAC (for Multiple Access Computer, the actual system that was developed, as well as Machine Aided Cognition, the larger goal of the project) led to the development of time-sharing, where multiple networked display stations maintain simultaneous access to a large computer through separate ports of entry. In this photo from a computer conference of 1968 between MIT and the Technical University of Berlin, the diagram shows the transatlantic cable routes used to connect a Berlin terminal with a time-sharing computer in MIT.

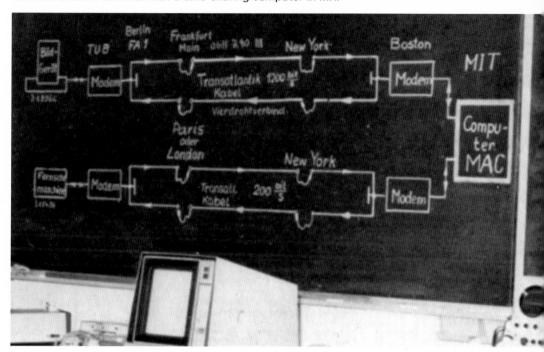

28. Stone-age CAD graphics from MIT's Kludge, 1964. Computer Aided Design followed directly from the work done on N/C. "The Kludge" (nicknamed from technical slang for a motley set of components somehow jury-rigged into working properly) was the first practical solution to the problem of computer graphics interface.

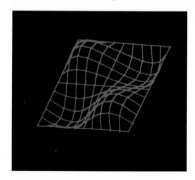 

29. Henry Fonda as the President who ordered the nuclear annihilation of New York City, in *Fail-Safe*, dir. Sidney Lumet. "We are responsible. We let our machines get out of control."

Stress

The skills of the artisan machinist, because they are located within the density of the individual's bodily experience and not translated into an abstracted and numerical context, provide a quotient of viscosity, an obstacle to frictionless flow in the circuit of information capital. And yet, as is still the case in the aeronautics industry, production systems have not advanced enough to transfer all skilled labor to the machine and thereby realize the dream of the workerless factory. In the illustration of the sectioned helicopter blade rotor, the agonistic boundary between the expanding domain of the N/C machine and the skill reservoir of the artisan machinist is evident.

Flexible specialization on the work floor divides workers into two categories: the skilled, whose specialized knowledge, for example, in running automated machines makes them a core asset of the company; and the unskilled, who are in a less stable position today than under the Fordist regime because of the diminished power of organized labor. Within the Fordist regime, the labor union had worked both to regulate supply and demand (by making it possible for workers to consume commodities and thus guarding against the very real threat

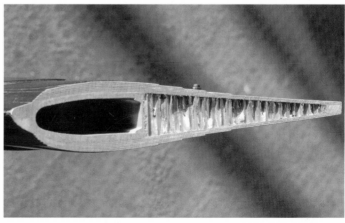

30. Sectioned rotor.

31. Belgian striker, 1960

The social control of large groups was unquestioningly mediated by the so-called Keynesian consensus between state, management, and unions. After World War II, the Western countries went through 20 years of steady growth, carrying out the Keynesian-influenced policies of the New Deal in the United States and those adopted by European states, which tied increases in wages to increases in labor marginal productivity. Keynes justified spending by the State to counter the "exogenous shock" of unemployment. Abandoning the neoclassical quantity theory of money and the labor-market theory of employment, these theories relied on a conception of long-term equilibrium operating within economies: that unemployment and other crises were only moments of disequilibrium caused by inequalities in supply and demand functions. As such, labor demands for wages above the "natural" level set by the economy could set off unemployment. Governmental intervention was likewise seen as a disequilibrating force. In any case, the neoclassical theorist would view such crises as "short-term" disruptions, passing as the economy returned to equilibrium.

Perhaps Keynes' most critical move was the denial of long-term equilibrium. This denial became the foundation of his principle of effective demand, according to which the level of employment as well as prices is determined by expected demand for output (along of overproduction) and to better mobilize the work force. The economies of scale introduced by Fordism and its mass-production facilities brought together large groups of workers into concentrated areas. Protecting against the dangers of the "open mass" required new methods of controlling large groups. The mechanisms of the "Keynesian consensus," which fostered class awareness and solidarity among workers, though in a way that served to integrate them further into the production process, increased the power of labor unions.

In the decade after World War II, and in the wake of wartime wage freezes, no-strike bans, and the growth of labor union power, the United States experienced the most intense period of strikes in the country's history. Management forces responded with two general strategies. Many factories were relocated from the city to the suburbs, which served to break down the group identification fostered within the urban milieu. Management also aggressively pursued a program

with supply conditions). Here Keynes shifts the determining factor in employment from long-term equilibria to an idea of short-term equilibria. The wages demanded by labor are no longer a determinant of employment levels, as in the labor-market theory, but are macroeconomic outcomes over which labor has little control. If effective demand is too low, unemployment will result regardless of the actions of labor. Hence, if the producers' demand is met without reaching full employment, a condition of unemployment equilibrium can be reached. This equilibrium could not be broken by reducing wages, as a drop in wages would result in a drop in effective demand. The state is then justified in its role as an arbitrator between labor and management and in the use of government spending as an "exogenous shock" to ward off the effects of structural unemployment by increasing effective demand. "The increase in effective demand will, generally speaking, spend itself partly in increasing the quantity of employment and partly in raising the level of prices. Thus instead of constant prices in conditions of unemployment, and of prices rising in proportion to the quantity of money in conditions of full employment, we have in fact a condition of prices rising gradually as employment increases."[16]

32. Norbert Weiner feeding back.

For management, there were two difficulties in the Keynesian system: the loss of control over the production process with the validation of unions, and the "regulation crises" in equilibrating the supply-and-demand relation, including the oversaturation of the domestic market for consumer goods, the availability of cheaper overseas labor, and the growing lack of consumer satisfaction with mass-produced goods. Yet underneath Keynesian policies, the new modalities of control available with the invention of cybernetic and information technologies provided a way out, both enhancing control over labor and dealing with the regulation crises. As early as 1949, Norbert Weiner, the founder of the science of cybernetics, saw the danger of the new kinds of control available through these technologies and aligned himself with the struggles of labor. In a letter written that year to the United Auto Worker's Walter Reuther, Weiner argued that "any labor which is in competition with slave labor, whether the slaves are human or mechanical, must accept the conditions of work of slave labor." For

54

of industrial automation to further solidify its control of the factory. These developments signaled a sharp decline both in the labor union and in the role of labor itself within the production process.

New forms of control within factories were also introduced, following the pandemonic imperative to promote environments of local intelligence over the Fordist and Taylorist citadels of global information control. While Ford and Taylor were instrumental in abstracting the labor process, the "rationalism" of their modes of control led them to analyze the problem of labor in a sense analogous to the dictates of a central processing unit; that is, both analyzed and imposed solutions from above. "Neo-Fordist" developments, whether refered to as flexible specialization, just-in-time production, or lean production, have emphasized the "bounded rationality" of those overseeing the labor process and recognized that even workers themselves must be able to diag-

Weiner, this kind of control was only too susceptible to exploitation by "a certain type of businessman and a certain type of military man to get rid once and for all of the labor unions, of all forms of socialization, and of all restrictions to individual profiteering."[17]

The period of Keynesian policies served only as a holding pattern, a stop gap, allowing the new production techniques to take hold gradually, to develop and refine themselves, while alleviating the massive social unrest that might have resulted with sudden, sweeping changes. It is during this period that flux and change became the tools of power relations. Following the crises of regulation, these technologies set the stage for the abandonment of the Keynesian consensus. The technique employed involved the subsumption of productive elements within the controlled and regulated time of the cybernetic machine, to emerge as semi-autonomous entities or demons: the slave labor already clearly intuited by Weiner.

nose problems on the fly. In this way, decision-making in production ceased to be a strictly top-down affair and grew to incorporate the factory floor as a whole.

Yet this shift should not be seen as "empowerment." The new mental or nervous discipline required of the worker, now invested with a small and carefully defined degree of initiative and local intelligence, has generated new techniques of surveillance and control aimed at extracting initiative from the worker. An example of the more astonishing of such control devices is the insidious Andon board, developed as part of the Toyota company's strategy of lean production. This method was introduced in the mid-80s in the United States in a joint venture between Toyota and Chevrolet, the New United Motors Manufacturing, Inc. (NUMMI), in California. The Andon board is an electronic display unit in which each worker's station is represented as a rectangular box. If the pace on the line becomes too great, the worker is instructed to pull a cord, causing that station to light up on the central board. The overseers, however, whose job it is to analyze all the data passing through the device, do not seek to keep the lights from flashing. The lights, on the contrary, are meant to be constantly flashing as management continually stresses the system, searching for ways to extract ever more worker productivity. Such a situation might be characterized as hyper-Taylorist; its aim is not only to measure, abstract, and quantify the motions made by workers, but to do so using techniques of local distributed intelligence, continually verifying whether the system is able to return to equilibrium. The data thus generated do not make claims for universal applicability, as did those generated by Taylor, but seeks to exert maximum pressure on the local system to discover its own limit.

33. The Pandemonic Sublime: "Double Speed." Larry Poons, 1962
71x139 in., coll. Frank Stella.

"Management by stress" is how Mike Parker and Jane Slaughter characterize the productive apparatus surrounding the Andon board. They deny claims that the system operates through a democratic process of teamwork absent from Taylorist models.[18] In truth, "teamwork" itself belongs to a more systematic strategy of extracting increasing amounts of work from the worker. For instance, if a worker is absent or working slowly, the team must make up for this deficiency, creating powerful peer pressure on efficiency and timeliness. Workers are encouraged to take part in "quality circles" on their own time to discuss ways of improving the production process. While this may appear, and is certainly presented as, empowering (giving the worker more responsibility), it must be remembered that teams have no control over the work process itself. Further, with respect to Taylorism, lean production retains, even enhances, the painstaking cataloging and specification of each gesture and motion the worker must use to complete a given task. "Teamwork" effectively raises Taylorism to the collec-

tive level, subsumes workers more fully within the process of production, and utilizes their nervous systems to the highest possible extent by investing workers with a feeling of responsibility for a production process over which they have no say. A manual distributed at a Michigan Mazda plant reads: "If you are standing at your machine doing nothing, you are not gaining respect as a human being." The benefits of this system for management are many: decreased absenteeism, increased productivity, and more pliable workers. Lean production works in concert with "just in time" inventory control, technology that minimizes indirect labor (warehousing, etc.), extensive use of subcontracting, and continuous speedup. All these techniques serve to put each part of the production process into a continuous state of stress. In effect, an "economy of stress" is being created, with all available time placed in the interest of maximizing production. Here decentralization moves capital into a time-based regime as the Keynesian consensus is eclipsed.

34. Andon board at work, NUMMI factory.

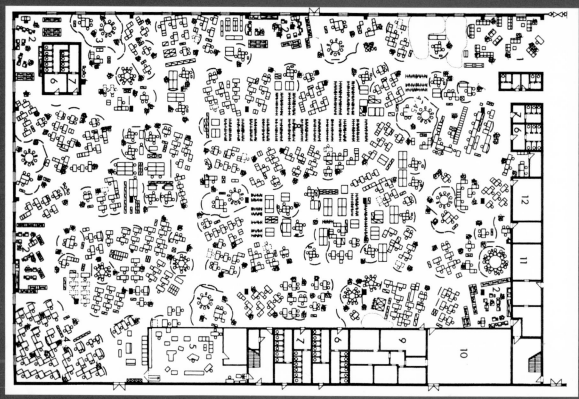

35. Pandemonium on the floor: a typical landscape plan from the
German Quickborner Team. GEG-Versand in Kamen, Germany, 1963-4.

Bürolandschaft

With the late 1950s invention of Bürolandschaft, or office landscaping, the Quickborner Team für Planung und Organisation, a management consulting group based in a suburb of Hamburg, precipitated a fundamental shift in the design of the office environment. Like most of the significant designs of the late twentieth century, the office landscape was formulated to meet the needs of abstract organizational and bureaucratic criteria. In the pure formation of spaces, the project of freeing the flows of information capital had the general effect of transforming places into zones of homogeneity and complete malleability. By dissolving the walls of the traditional office building with its myriad small, private offices and central corridors, in favor of vast open spaces populated by whirling workstations, the Quickborner team recast the office as a dynamic parallel processing machine.

The connections between the various nodes of the office were enhanced, quickening the tempo of information exchange and greatly increasing the surveillance power of management. The apparent chaos of Quickborner's office plans belies the fact that the team used no less than 68 rules to generate the

36. Departmental groupings and 37. Circulation paths in the Osram building in Munich, Germany. Planned by the Quickborner Team, 1962–63.

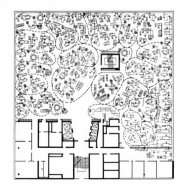 

desired configurations, strictly controlling environmental variables from acoustic levels to sight lines. The circulation between separate departments was painstakingly analyzed, resulting in diagrams with more than superficial resemblance to the demon hierarchy charts in Pandemonium architecture. The environment of the office landscape is shaped by communication flow, and capable, like conversations, of almost total flexibility and reconfiguration. The development of systems office furniture, beginning with Herman Miller's Action Office in 1964, further transformed the office into an infinitely flexible space, crossed with interchangeable nodes. Office workers must come to view themselves as part of a matrix, a metabolizing organization, of unrestricted universal capital. The worker is reconstructed as a demon or sub-routine within the disciplinary matrix, and further reconstructed individually and physically through the use of ergonomic systems furniture that anticipates his or her movements with precleared, frictionless pathways.

Mirroring the evolution of decentralized control in the factory, the new disciplinary matrix of the information office first passed through a phase of centralization. This was driven by both technical and social refinements: the refinement of interchangeable part production, which allowed the widespread distribution of devices such as the typewriter, and the refinement of the large-scale centralized techniques of administration, as formalized by Taylor. The "American Open Plan," the spatial analog to this sociotechnical regime, gathered workers who had once been in small, walled offices into a single large workspace with identical workstations aligned on a grid (see ills. 38 and 39). This technique of space-making allowed both the routinization of office work (which would generally move in a linear fashion through the office, much like an assembly line) and the creation of a new type of office worker (which was reflected demographically in the mass migration of women into the almost exclusively male vocation of office work). No longer separated into individual offices, the new worker would become both symbolically and effectively absorbed within a vast "pool" of workers who would collectively, rather than individually, carry out tasks. The shift to decentralized control in office environments, as exemplified in Bürolandschaft, heralds a new type of office collective, an information age collective, forced by the greater need for fluidity and innovation to free itself of the exclusive top-down control and rigid grid of the Open Plan.

The **Bürolandschaft model** represents the moment of take-off, one which has culminated in the virtual office of today, with its indefinite extension through the use of modems, fax machines, portable computers, pagers, voice mail, and cellular telephones.

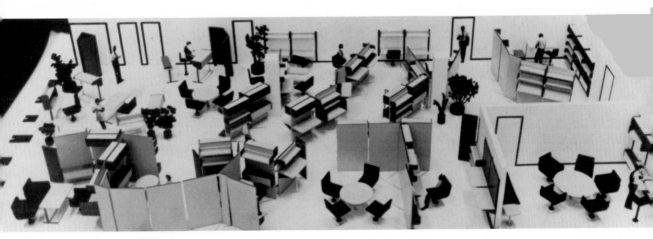

38. Scale model of Herman Miller Action Office.

39. Anthony Perkins as K. in *The Trial*, dir. Orson Wells, 1962.
40. The Larkin Building atrium, Frank Lloyd Wright, 1903.

41. Toward a New Architecture: CRT, white-noise generator, and plant.
Herman Miller's Action Office system.

In the Bürolandschaft model, the logic behind the reorganized social field is one of dispersal. Indeed, its planners attempted nothing short of creating a place solely from the demands of expediting "communication flow." Distractions—visual, aural, and tactile, an element of friction in the flow of communication—were removed: visually through indirect sight-lines, movable screens and plants, light file carts used to minimize the clutter of paper and other stored items, and carefully controlled lighting conditions and neutral colors; aurally through carpeting, the isolation of noisy equipment, and the use of various "white noise" devices; and temporally by placing those departments which interact most frequently closest to one another, in order to minimize circulation time, and through the use of light furniture and portable screens (which carry ducts for electricity and communications systems), so that the office may be quickly reformulated to fit the changing needs of communication flow.[19]

Indeed an almost haptic sense of continuity is called for through the preference for "large, open, and unencumbered" spaces, with a minimum of 100 people per room: a uniformity of space, reduced to a single tactile, visual, and aural dimension, so that the only apparent differences are those which have to do with the imperatives of communication and organizational flow. It is, in a sense, the fulfillment of the potentials of "universal space" which some persist in viewing, like instrumental rationality, as a wholly neutral development of modernism. In Bürolandschaft planning universal space (in the use of modularity, the blank curtain wall, the uninterrupted floor slab) amounts to a certain kind of sensory deprivation, a genericality which does not bespeak the opening up of potentials and the lack of regulation, but rather the dissolution of the *workplace-as-citadel*—a process that more fully embeds workers within the directed temporal aspects of communication flow.

In this transition from workplace-as-citadel to workplace-as-environment, design is not used to signify hierarchy or the operation of power: hierarchy is constituted by the way one moves through the office environment, by the pathways one takes. The office becomes *performative*, an environment created in the process of moving through it; the office could be said

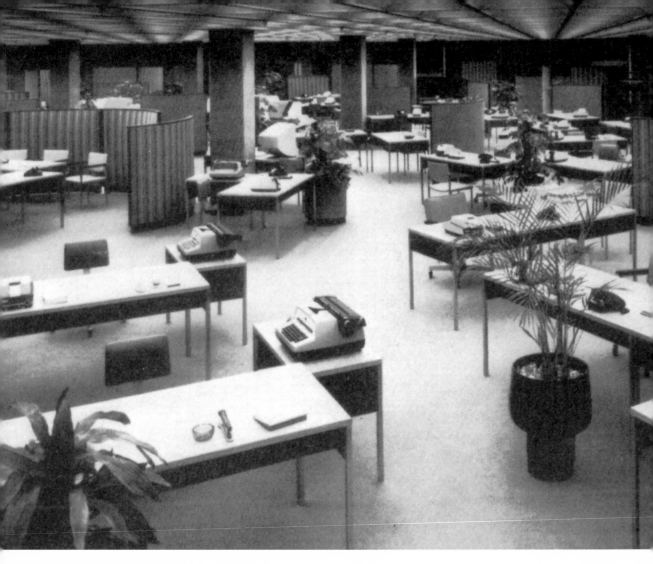

42. An early test floor in the US: Eastman Kodak in 1967, by the
Quickborner team.

to *individuate* its workers on the basis of this movement. This distinction can be seen in a larger, urban context as well: one's position within the social hierarchy has much to do with how one communicates (the technological devices one uses, for instance) and how one moves through increasingly dispersed urban and suburban environments. In this Bürolandschaft urbanism, skilled workers and system analysts, on the one hand, and mobile unskilled workers, on the other, move through separate superimposed cities, a sort of placeless and artificial provincialism based on one's position within systems of postindustrial production. For Manuel Castells, this is the space of production engendered through information-technology manufacturing; it is the "milieu of innovation," which is "able to generate within itself a continuous flow of the key elements that constitute the basis for innovative production of information technologies, namely: new scientific and technological information, high risk capital, and innovative technical labor." In the environment of constant innovation, communication is all important: "there is little need of spatial proximity because of transportation costs; but there is much need to be able to exchange personal views on last night's software breakthrough, or on a recent trip to Japan."[20] The postindustrial city, mobile and malleable, operating as a distributed system of enclaves, can be seen as a device for the creation of workers within this milieu, for fostering the sense of constrained individualism necessary to their functioning within conditions where they must display controlled forms of intelligence and innovation. The dispersion of forms in the contemporary urban fabric, seen for example in the contemporary city's multiple or nonexistent centers, is possible only through the creation of a common connecting fabric, a kind of information-time that binds objects as performative constituents of a distributed system. In this sense, the figures in the landscape have given way to the landscape itself.

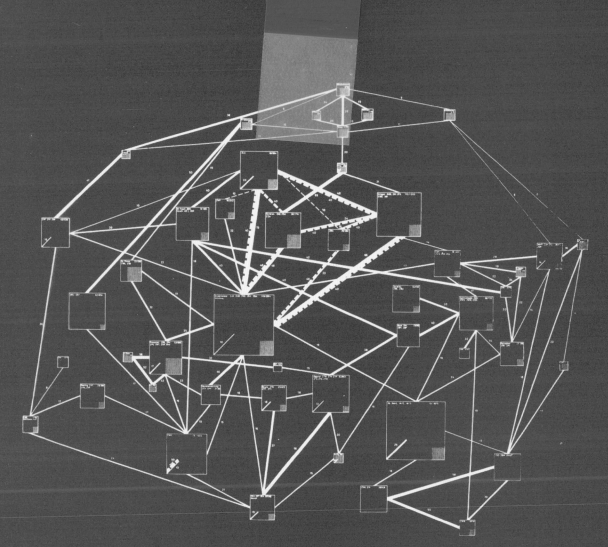

43. Organizational interaction diagram, Quickborner Team.

Distributed system

The landscape of production is now a massively parallel set of interconnected distributed systems. In the diagram generated by the Quickborner Team as part of the planning process for the layout of an office landscape (illus. no. 43), the boxes represent departments or equipment, while the lines between them indicate the relative intensity of the interactions between departments. These diagrams were created to abstract the patterns of communication flow from the configuration of the office, manipulated as idealized space plans, then fitted to actual available space to create plan layouts. But could this diagram not just as easily refer to any number of dehierarchized organizations (the network of suppliers, producers and distributors in just-in-time manufacturing, the flow of currency between trading centers, a heterarchy of demons within a Pandemonic system) which are directed through shared protocols, interconnections, and directed rates of flow? Diagrams of communication flow are the abstract formulations of the distributed systems which form the dominant environment of the second half of the twentieth century. These distributed systems are driven by a new set of organizational strategies; the signs of their existence are manifold, the scope of their effects pervasive.

As compunication technologies drastically increase the amount of information available for gathering and filtering, and as new forms of organization subsequently become available, the economy is driven to become a distributed system. Just as the military realized during World War II the primary importance of decentralized command and communications systems in complex battlefield situations, the expanding presence of information (whether in the growing complexity of networked financial institutions, massive demographic research databases, or techniques of production and distribution) has brought into focus the sheer complexity of interactions which make up an economy and the subsequent need for dehierarchized, localized tactics to apprehend and direct these interactions. And just as the chaos of battle became harnessed to fluid, platoon-style command structures, so has the chaos of information been harnessed to the imperatives of market institutions.

This new bond between information and market institutions, a link which is at the heart of contemporary neoconservative economic theory, was forged by the Austrian School of Economics, founded by Carl Menger in 1870. Menger

44. Where have all the managers gone? The eleventh floor of Mies' Toronto Dominion Center, originally designed for executive and managerial cadres, was nearly vacated when the managers moved down into their departments. The decision to place management on the eleventh floor, at the very center of the bank's operations, was itself a departure from the traditional (vertical) logic of spatial hierarchy, which would have put management on the top (54th) floor. Pictured here in 1968, the eleventh floor is now reserved for executives and the display of art.

argued that market order, like the evolution of law and language, was the unintended, spontaneous result of myriad human actions and historical events. Centralized planned economies of the socialist (and later Keynesian) type thus were untenable: the fullest economic use of resources, he argued, occurs only through a laissez-faire market price system, applied not only to final products, but to intermediate ones as well. Drawing an explicit analogy between social and natural orders, the Austrian School viewed the market as coordinating economic factors through mutual adaptation, like the functioning of a biological organism. While the use of biological analogy is not in itself novel (Adam Smith spoke of the natural price toward which prices will tend, and Turgot compared the circulation of money with the circulation of blood, both in 1776), what is new is the conception (extended and sytematized by the most brilliant protegés of the Austrian School, Joseph Schumpeter and Friedrich von Hayek) of *spontaneous order* within an economic environment of complexity and disequilibrium.

This conception of the regulatory powers of the market should not be seen as a reformulation of a classical argument for laissez-faire policies based on equilibrium theories of market regulation, such as Jean-Baptiste Say's law of the automatic balance of supply and demand (1803). Classical and neoclassical economic theory conceived of the market as an equilibrating force only temporarily disrupted by "exogenous" forces such as political unrest. The modeling of economic theory here treats men and materials as perfectly mobile entities and considers the dissemination of information to be frictionless and unobstructed. Indeed, the mathematical economist Leon Walras, who elegantly demonstrated a process of successive approximations, or *tâtonnement* (trial-and-error groping), by which partial equilibria could give rise to a "general equilibrium" that could not have been predicted in advance, viewed private property as *resistant* to the smooth functioning of the market; so that Walrasian thought became the theoretical basis for a form of market socialism. For this reason, the Austrian School viewed Walras' "pure and perfect competition" as an imaginary construction which in actuality banishes competition from the market.

With the realization that information could be treated as a fluid material came the logistical attempt to maximize the speed of information processing and transmission. On the scale of economies, in the working of the global market, this program is executed as the attempt to make economic factors fluid so that they may be better coordinated. For Friedrich von Hayek, perhaps the father of neoconservative economics, the solution to the problem of the imperfect dissemination of information is to make it a commodity: information is more fully exploited when subjected to market conditions. Social and economic formations are complex and environmental; like pandemonium demons, people follow abstract, localized rules, ignorant of the movement of the whole, yet their actions are coordinated through the operation of the market. Ironically, perhaps, the "spontaneous order" so praised by Hayek and Menger for its liberating potential would only further the range of control available to bureaucratic and institutional interests. The market here is transformed from a static mechanism for the exchange of goods into an accelerator, a dynamic mechanism for the mobilization of information capital.

45. A bad time in Patagonia: mountain-climbing, along with other "extreme" sports, forsakes reliance on geometrically fixed rules typified by traditional sport, seeking instead that zone of intimately sensing and reacting to an ever-changing, potentially hostile environment. Werner Herzog's *Scream of Stone*, 1991.

As early as 1911, Joseph Schumpeter realized that the economic mobilization of information would require a conceptual framework different from that of the neoclassical equilibrium model. "Development in our sense [the creation of information] is a distinct phenomenon, entirely foreign to what may be observed in the circular flow or in the tendency toward equilibrium. It is spontaneous and discontinuous change in the channels of the flow, disturbance of equilibrium, which forever alters and displaces the equilibrium state previously existing."[21] Whereas the concept of equilibrium contains formal qualities which allow the movement of the system to be known rationally, the economics of disequilibrium have tended to

privilege the freedom of the market precisely for the fact that its operations are unknown and inaccessible. Hence, Hayek's arguments defending the market against central planning and government intervention are based not on notions of rationality, but ignorance.[22] Schumpeter, however, departed from the Austrian School with a theme that in a sense haunted him throughout his career: what he saw pessimistically as the decline of capitalism (which he always associated with the heroic figure of the entrepreneur) through bureaucratization, in a process leading ultimately to socialism.[24] While the bureaucratization of innovation has indeed occurred (particularly in information technology), Schumpeter (who died in 1950) was

46. Schumpeter at Harvard, 1948
47. Hayek puts his final touches on *The Constitution of Liberty* in the Alps

unaware of the burgeoning, fluid bureaucratic techniques which would soon come to define the postwar world. This technologically mediated decentralization, which led to the success of the kind of social control referred to by Gaudemar as the "institutionalization of fluctuation," has turned innovation into an organizational imperative.

As in pandemonium computer architecture, agents move across the economic landscape, performing functions and following rules, without access to the behavior of the whole system. It is precisely this ignorance of the system that allows the system to function optimally, bringing about unintended benefits that could not have been rationally predicted. Lack of prediction does not mean lack of control; Hayek includes cybernetics as "a special discipline which is also concerned with what are called self-organizing or self-generating systems." Neo-conservative economics conceives of these agents as operating within a common network—the market—which coordinates actions in terms of mutual consistency and provides vital means of control. For an economist like Gary Becker, then, it is possible to subsume all human actions and relationships under the sign of economic actions and relationships, justified by the primal need of "maximizing behavior." The market, now pandemonic in scope and effect, spontaneously allows the "optimal or rational accumulation of costly information."[24]

The discovery of the viscosity of information and the bounded rationality of heuristics, together with the growing importance of research and development (and of knowledge in general) to industry and cybernetics and compunication networks, has transformed the market into a colonizing force. The now self-propelling market continually extends its inherent systems of abstraction into previously inviolate territories, rendering all surfaces (communication interfaces, the boundary between idea and matter, spatial and temporal relationships) subject to its modulations and control, within a system of fluid command hierarchies and interconnections. The history of distributed systems corresponds precisely to that of the market, and one need only study the effects of these systems—highways and airports, advanced credit institutions, global corporations, suburbs and televisions—on the formation of the city, the global order, and life itself, to see the transformation wrought by the flow of abstract information.

Distributed systems require for their operation a homogenous standard of inter-connectivity. This protocol endows the distributed system with what we have been calling its environmental quality and with the corresponding property of closeness, the ability to be all-encompassing, totalizing, absorptive, and dena-turing. This is in sharp contrast to the city as a citadel or cluster of citadels, which creates distinct subject relations, maintains separation and distance, and is constructive and differentiating. As the market relentlessly expands its grip upon the city, moving both outward toward new territory and inward to parse that which it has already absorbed, the city itself, as a locus of human culture, as a distinct and separate citadel structure, disintegrates.

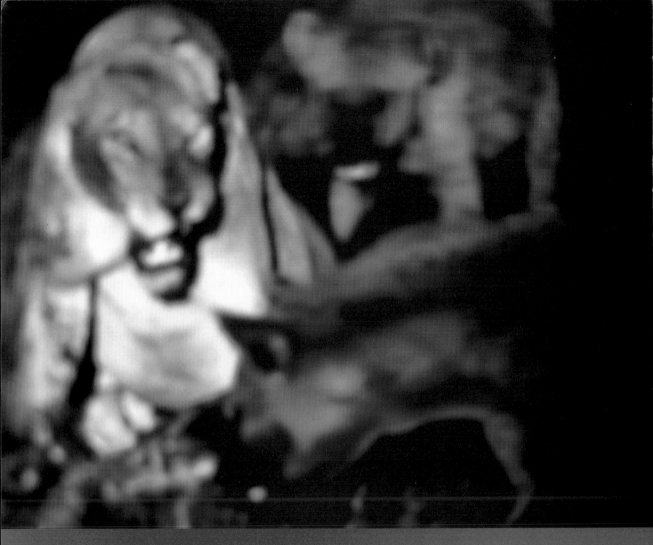

48. Masters of the arts of havoc and spontaneous cooperative behavior,
a clan of spotted hyenas mob a lone lion, driving it from its kill.

Predation

As information is increasingly subsumed as a commodity—medium within capital and as compunication systems continue to provide a venue for the ever accelerating transmission of information and social relations of capital to populations of unprecedented size and dispersal, the tasks of information processing are being dramatically recast. Under a market system whose mode of being proceeds through expansion and increasing mobilization, the more easily disseminated forms of information will be selected and privileged over those that resist easy translation into the digital realm of compunicational abstraction. By subsuming the flow of information to its own ends and in the absence of citadel formations such as a state apparatus, the market itself now achieves a new means of social control. Control may now be exercised simply through the exposure of information to market forces, that is, through the transvaluation of information into a commodity, refashioning it at the moment of its abstraction to fit the computational milieu.

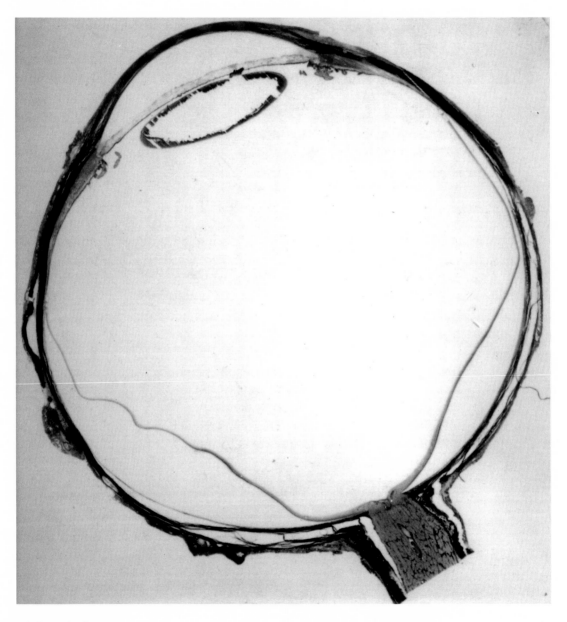

49. Detached retina.

The Pandemonic Eye is a predator, embedding its rapacious logic ever more deeply into the social fold. It is constantly and relentlessly expanding, apprehending and assimilating new prey, driven by the feedback loops of a capitalist enterprise availing itself of vast amounts of cheap energy, enlarged (yet supple) scales of production, and ever faster and more intermeshed telecommunications and information-processing systems. What remains is the blurring of all citadel structures, from the state, to the "aura" and authority of works of art, to the solemn autonomy of the ego, within the expanding and directed environment of information capital. It is the drama of unique existence constantly supplanted by the universal equality of things. And as we are not held in thrall so much anymore to law, to de jure formations and judicial enforcement, as we are to the de facto methods by which we communicate and the technological, social, and economic forces that shape this communication, our attempts to carve out a space of freedom by diverting communication flow must be aimed at the level of communication infrastructure, and at the processes by which this infrastructure determines the shape of our social worlds.

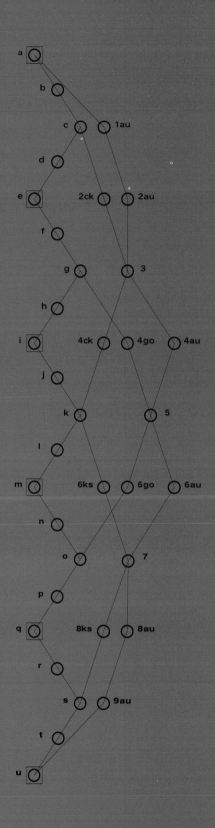

A Word About the Font

Branden Hookway

Information technology, since the days of the Bauhaus and the postwar Swiss schools, has begun subtly but profoundly to transform the role of the designer from that of simply maximizing clarity (scientific universality of expression) to that of differentiating and modulating processes and events in the ongoing stream of form-production. In typography, the earlier orders were quickly subsumed within the new: Helvetica (1957) and Univers (1954) have become emblems of the 60s corporate culture for which they were created, their "clarity" now but another stylistic feature among others available to the designer. These developments mirror the migration of rationalization in culture from the production of specific forms to the infrastructural systems which govern form production itself.

The 36 Pandemonium fonts are based on Helvetica, Univers, and other letter-forms of the same corporate family. While they make use of a limited morphology, their specific form shifts throughout the book, blending into and across one another according to the pathways shown in the diagram on the left. Like the *Bürolandschaft*, the fonts combine a banal modernist vocabulary with a mobile organizational structure to produce an "environment" rather than a fixed form. In this case, the diagram loops in upon itself, moving resolutely, but toward no finite end—systematized difference once again zero-sums itself as non-difference. A measure of serif is added to the mix to maximize the agonistic tension.

Works Cited

1. Daniel Bell, "Teletext and Technology: New Networks of Knowledge and Information in Postindustrial Society" in *The Winding Passage* (Cambridge, MA: ABT Books, 1980) pg. 39. This landmark article, originally printed in *Encounter* (London), XLVIII, no.6 (June 1977), was drawn from a larger manuscript, "The Social Framework of an Information Society," prepared for the Laboratory of Computer Science at MIT in 1975 and printed in Michael Dertouzos and Joel Moses, *The Computer Age: A Twenty Year View* (Cambridge, MA: MIT Press, 1975). The essay was funded by AT&T, IBM, the Office of Naval Research, and MIT, and was reprinted in revised form in *Encounter*, a London-based journal with which Bell had been associated since the 50s and which was one of the earliest forums for neo-conservative ideas. Encounter was hit by scandal in 1967 when it was revealed that it, along with several other similar journals as well as the Congress of Cultural Freedom, had received covert funding from the CIA. (On the Encounter affair, see Frank Kermode, "Life at Encounter," *Partisan Review* 62 [Fall 1996], pp. 661–73; and Neil Berry, "Encounter," *Antioch Review* 51 [Spring 1993], pp. 194–211.)

2. Michael J. Piore and Charles E. Sabel, *The Second Industrial Divide: Possibilities for Prosperity* (New York: Basic Books, 1984).

3. On the new crisis economy, see Eric Alliez and Michel Feher, "The Luster of Capital," in Michel Feher and Sanford Kwinter, eds., *ZONE 1|2: The Contemporary City* (New York: Zone Books, 1986). A global perspective is discussed in Samir Amin, *Capitalism in the Age of Globalization: The Management of Contemporary Society* (London: Zed Books, 1997).

4. Walter Benjamin, "The Work of Art in the Age of Mechanical Reproduction," in Hannah Arendt, ed. *Illuminations* (New York: Schocken, 1973).

5. Manuel De Landa, *War in the Age of Intelligent Machines* (New York: Swerve Editions, Zone Books, 1991) p.206.

6. Oliver G. Selfridge and Ulric Neisser, "Pattern Recognition by Machine," *Scientific American* (August 1960), pp. 60–68. See also Oliver G. Selfridge, "Pandemonium: A Paradigm for Learning," in James A. Anderson and Edward Rosenfeld, eds. *Neurocomputing* (Cambridge, Mass.: MIT Press, 1988), which was originally printed in *Mechanisation of Thought Processes: Proceedings of a Symposium Held at the National Physics Laboratory* (London: HMSO, 1958).

7. Daniel Dennett, *Consciousness Explained* (New York: Back Bay Books, 1991), p. 263.

8. *The RAND Corporation: The First Fifteen Years* (Santa Monica, CA: RAND Corporation, 1963). Quoted from pp. 2, 3, 27, 26.

9. Figures on MIT were taken from Dorothy Nelkin, *The University and Military Research: Moral Politics at M.I.T.* (Ithaca: Cornell University Press, 1972). Quotes are from Karl L. Wildes and Nilo A. Lindgren, *A Century of Electrical Engineering and Computer Science at MIT, 1882–1982* (Cambridge, MA: The MIT Press, 1985), pp. 283, 300. See also John Burchard, *Q.E.D: M.I.T. in World War II* (New York: John Wiley & Sons, 1948).

10. Herbert A. Simon, "Rational Choice and the Structure of the Environment" (1956), in Herbert A. Simon, *Models of Thought* (New Haven: Yale University Press, 1979).

11. Gilles Deleuze and Felix Guattari, *A Thousand Plateaus: Capitalism & Schizophrenia*, tr. Brian Massumi (Minneapolis: University of Minnesota Press, 1987), p. 458.

12. Jean-Paul de Gaudemar, "The Mobile Factory," tr. Alyson Waters, in Michel Feher and Sanford Kwinter, eds., *ZONE 1|2: The Contemporary City* (New York: Zone Books, 1986), p. 291.

13. On MIT's Servo Lab and the Whirlwind computer, see Wildes and Lindgren, pp. 210–235. A detailed account of the development of numerical control and subsequent related technologies at MIT may be found in J. Francis Reintjes, *Numerical Control: Making a New Technology* (New York: Oxford University Press, 1991).

14. David F. Noble, *Forces of Production: A Social History of Industrial Automation* (New York: Alfred A. Knopf, 1984).

15. David F. Noble, "Command Performance: A Perspective on Military Enterprise and Technological Change," in Merritt Roe Smith, ed., *Military Enterprise and Technological Change* (Cambridge, MA: MIT Press, 1985). The quotes in the main text are from Lieutenant General C.S. Irvine, "Keynote Address," Proceedings of the Electronics Industries Association Symposium, 1957, quoted in Jeremy Rifkin, *The End of Work* (New York: G.P. Putnam's Sons, 1993), pp. 182–83.

16. Quoted in W.W. Rostow, *Theorists of Economic Growth from David Hume to the Present* (New York: Oxford University Press, 1990), p. 610 n. 73. The original source is J.M. Keynes, *The General Theory of Employment, Interest, and Money* (London: MacMillan, 1936), p. 296. On the Keynsian consensus, cf. Alliez and Feher, "The Luster of Capital."

17. Original source: Norbert Weiner, letters to Walter Reuther, August 13, 1949, and July 26, 1950, *Wiener Papers*, MIT archives. Quoted in Noble, *Forces of Production*, pp. 76, 75.

18. See Mike Parker and Jane Slaughter, "Management by Stress," *Technology Review*, October 1988.

19. The Bürolandschaft approach developed by the Quickborner team, along with subsequent variations, is discussed in John Pile, *Open Office Planning* (London: The Architectural Press Ltd., 1978). See also Frank Duffy, *A New Approach to Office Planning* (London: Anbar Publications Ltd., 1966).

20. Manuel Castells, *The Informational City: Information, Technology, Economic Restructuring, and the Urban-Regional Process* (Oxford: Blackwell, 1989), p.88.

21. Joseph A. Schumpeter, *The Theory of Economic Development*, tr. Redvers Opie (Cambridge: Harvard University Press, 1955) p.63–64.

22. F. A. Hayek, *Law, Legislation, and Liberty, vol. 1, Rules and Order* (Chicago: University of Chicago Press, 1973) especially ch. 2.

23. Schumpeter's account of the decline of entrepreneurial capitalism is in his *Capitalism, Socialism and Democracy* (New York: Harper and Brothers, 1942).

24. Gary S. Becker, *The Economic Approach to Human Behavior* (Chicago: University of Chicago Press, 1974).

Photo Credits

Acknowledgements

Branden Hookway

I would like to thank: Lars Lerup, Albert Pope, Richard Wolin, and the Rice School of Architecture, for the atmosphere which nurtured the ideas here contained; Bruce Mau of/and Bruce Mau Design, whose studio vision shaped and directed this project at every step, making this a truly collaborative effort; and Sanford Kwinter, whose belief in this project (and countless promptings along the way) carried it through to completion.